SCHOLASTIC

AF650330

Exploring Social Studies 1

Name ______________________________

Class ______________________________

Photo attributions and credits:

p. 15: Fables; p. 27: Fables; p. 28: Fables; p. 29: Fables; pp. 32–36: Fables; pp. 38–40: Fables; pp. 42–45: Fables; p. 47: Fables; p. 49: Fables; p. 59: http://commons.wikimedia.org/wiki/File:BOXN_freight_action.jpg?uselang=en-gb by Sarbamit Chowdhury; p. 59: http://commons.wikimedia.org/wiki/File:Ship_Grietje.jpg?uselang=en-gb by Tvabutzku1234; p. 59: http://commons.wikimedia.org/wiki/File:Indian_Airlines.jpg?uselang=en-gb by Santanu Mondal; p. 60: Fables; p. 60: http://commons.wikimedia.org/wiki/File:DTC_Bus_Green_Non_AC.jpg?uselang=en-gb by Ramesh NG; p. 60: http://commons.wikimedia.org/wiki/File:Ambassador_taxi_in_tiumala.jpg by Tatiraju.rishabh; p. 60: http://commons.wikimedia.org/wiki/File:Honda_CBZ.jpg?uselang=en-gb by Neeks52x; p. 60: http://commons.wikimedia.org/wiki/File:Tata_Truck_India.jpg?uselang=en-gb by Adrian Sulc; p. 61: Fables; pp. 63–64: Fables.

First edition 2012
Reprinted 2012, 2013 (twice), 2014, 2015, 2016, 2017 (twice), 2019, 2022, 2024, 2026

ISBN 978-81-8477-935-6

Printed in India at Shiv Shakti Printing and Trading Co., Haryana

Contents

 ISBN 978-81-8477-935-6

Introduction

Exploring Social Studies is an exciting social studies series for levels 1 to 5. The books have been designed to fulfill the requirements of the National Curriculum Framework (NCF), which has been adopted by CBSE, ICSE and major State Educational Boards.

The series adopts a learner-centred approach, encouraging students to make connections between their role in their immediate environment and the world around them. The coursebooks are filled with lots of colourful photographs, maps and illustrations that expose students to real-life everyday experiences from around the world.

In addition, the series prepares students to meet the challenges of the future by
- following pyramidal pedagogy
- encouraging exploration and innovation
- facilitating observation and logical analysis to support conclusions
- promoting independent learning

Learn More provides activities that hone the students' ability to absorb, infer, classify, experiment and predict.

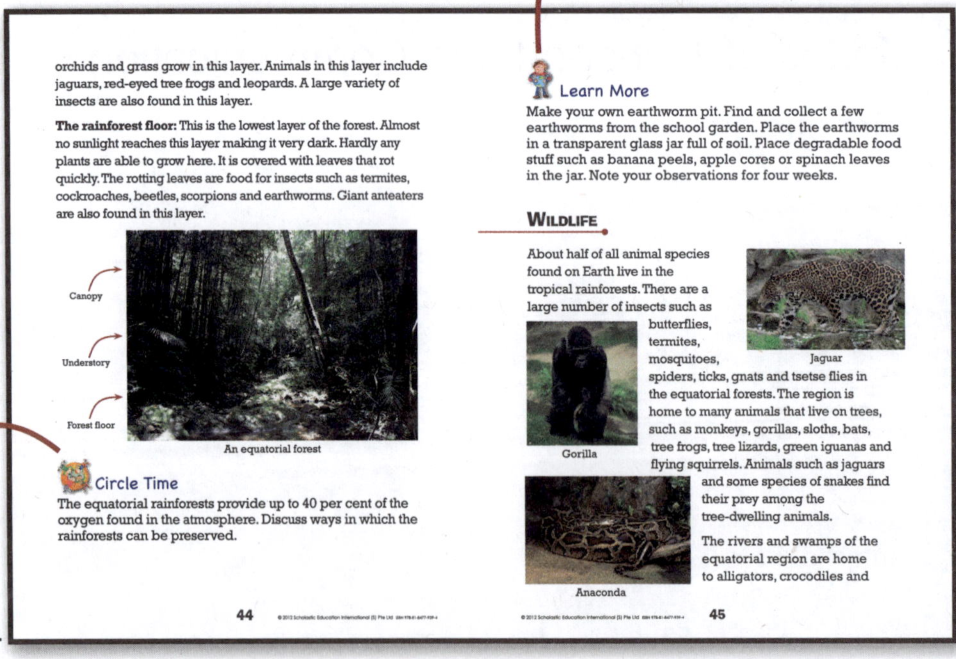
orchids and grass grow in this layer. Animals in this layer include jaguars, red-eyed tree frogs and leopards. A large variety of insects are also found in this layer.

The rainforest floor: This is the lowest layer of the forest. Almost no sunlight reaches this layer making it very dark. Hardly any plants are able to grow here. It is covered with leaves that rot quickly. The rotting leaves are food for insects such as termites, cockroaches, beetles, scorpions and earthworms. Giant anteaters are also found in this layer.

Canopy

Understory

Forest floor

An equatorial forest

Circle Time

The equatorial rainforests provide up to 40 per cent of the oxygen found in the atmosphere. Discuss ways in which the rainforests can be preserved.

44

Learn More

Make your own earthworm pit. Find and collect a few earthworms from the school garden. Place the earthworms in a transparent glass jar full of soil. Place degradable food stuff such as banana peels, apple cores or spinach leaves in the jar. Note your observations for four weeks.

WILDLIFE

About half of all animal species found on Earth live in the tropical rainforests. There are a large number of insects such as butterflies, termites, mosquitoes, spiders, ticks, gnats and tsetse flies in the equatorial forests. The region is home to many animals that live on trees, such as monkeys, gorillas, sloths, bats, tree frogs, tree lizards, green iguanas and flying squirrels. Animals such as jaguars and some species of snakes find their prey among the tree-dwelling animals.

Jaguar

Gorilla

The rivers and swamps of the equatorial region are home to alligators, crocodiles and

Anaconda

45

Circle Time promotes exchange of ideas and techniques while laying emphasis on working as a team.

 ISBN 978-81-8477-935-6

Learn More

On a map of India, mark the important industries and their location. Use an atlas as a guide.

Quiz Time

1. Fill in the blanks to complete the following sentences.
   a. Basket weaving is an example of a ______ industry.
   b. Most of the work in ______ industries is done by machines.
   c. Factories usually use ______ to manufacture finished goods.
   d. ______-scale industries employ a large number of people.
   e. Oil refineries are an example of a ______ industry.
2. Write short notes on the following.
   a. Large-scale industries
   b. Small-scale industries
   c. Cottage industries
3. Answer briefly.
   a. What are raw materials?
   b. What are the resources required to set up industries?
   c. What is the importance of human resources?

Why are large-scale industries not located in remote villages?

94

Factastic imparts interesting information and facts related to the topic under discussion.

Quiz Time tests knowledge retention and serves as a quick recap of the lesson.

Council conducts peace talks to maintain harmony. It sends peace-keeping forces to places affected by wars.

> **Factastic**
> Dr Nagendra Singh of India was the president of the International Court of Justice between 1985 and 1988.

The Economic and Social Council manages problems that are related to issues such as famine, drought, poverty and illiteracy.

The **International Court of Justice** settles legal disputes submitted by the member states.

The **Secretariat** maintains records and files of the meetings held by the UN. The head of the UN Secretariat is the **Secretary-General**.

> **Factastic**
> The UN headquarters is in New York City (USA); but the land on which it stands and the buildings it occupies are considered international territory. The European headquarters is in Switzerland. Other offices are in Vienna and Austria. The UN Economic Commissions are in Addis Ababa in Ethiopia, Amman in Jordan, Bangkok in Thailand and Santiago in Chile.

The UN has its own flag, post office as well as postage stamps. It has six official languages: Arabic, Chinese, English, French, Russian and Spanish.

The UN aims to develop and maintain cordial relations between member countries. It advocates peace throughout the world. The primary aim of the UN is to help eliminate disease, poverty and illiteracy from the world. It encourages nations to protect and preserve the environment. It also urges nations to work together with mutual respect for each other's rights.

cordial: courteous and gracious; friendly; warm
advocate: to speak or write in favour of; support or urge by argument; recommend publicly

137

Higher Order Thinking Skills (HOTS) questions are included in levels 4 and 5. These questions sharpen the students' skills of making inferences, understanding the logic behind a concept and thinking outside the box.

New and difficult words are defined in the **glossary**.

Circle Time

Have a discussion with your classmates about your favourite festival. Talk about what you like doing on this festival.

Explore

What do you do on Diwali? Tick (✓) the correct box.

	Yes	No
Burst noisy crackers that give out a lot of smoke.	☐	☐
Light sparklers and diyas with an adult.	☐	☐
Wear well-fitted, cotton clothes.	☐	☐
Visit friends and relatives.	☐	☐
Eat lots of sweets.	☐	☐
Decorate your house.	☐	☐

> **I Care...**
> While celebrating any festival, we must make sure that we do not disturb others.

Holi

Holi is one of the most popular Hindu festivals. It is the festival of colours. People put coloured powder and water on one another and eat sweets on Holi.

34

Explore encourages students to analyse and question.

I Care provides value education in levels 1 to 3.

Students are taught to use an atlas, an encyclopedia and the Internet in levels 3 to 5 to do basic research individually and in groups, to present reports and projects. These help build the students' ability to learn independently.

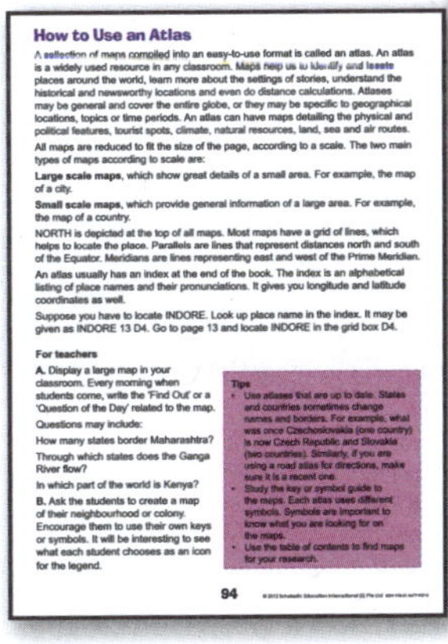
How to Use an Atlas

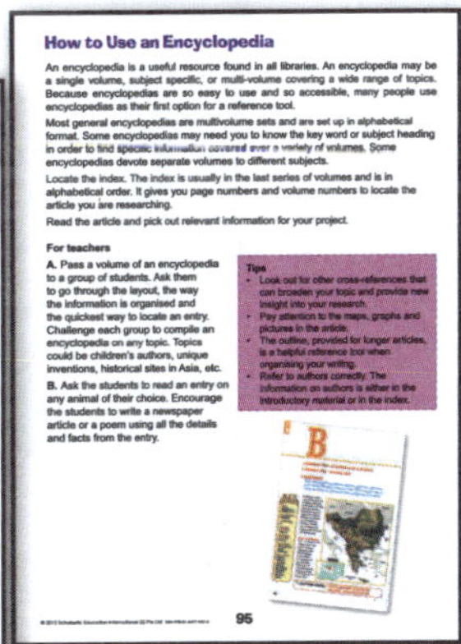
How to Use an Encyclopedia

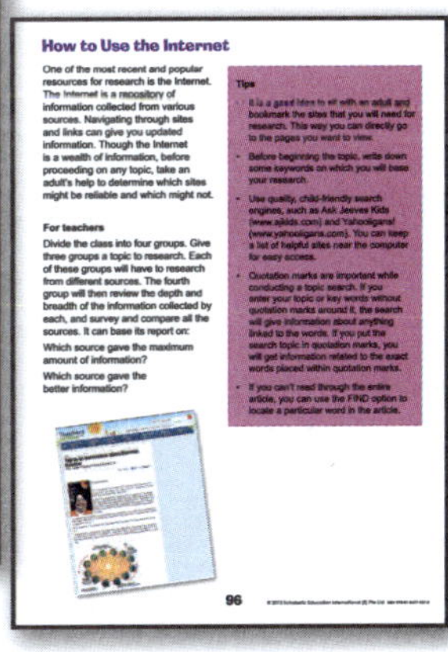
How to Use the Internet

 ISBN 978-81-8477-935-6

1 MYSELF

Welcome to your new class. Have you made any new friends in class? An easy way to get to know someone is by introducing yourself. Introducing yourself means telling people a little bit about yourself.

Complete the exercises given here and let your classmates find out a little about you.

My name is

______________.

I am ________ years old.

The name of my school is ________

____

______________.

Paste your photo here.

I study in class ________.

My father's name is

______________.

My mother's name is

______________.

I live in ______________ (city).

 ISBN 978-81-8477-935-6

Write or draw the things you like best.

My favourite colour is ____________.

My best friend is ____________.

I love listening to ____________.

My favourite TV show is ____________.

I love playing ____________.

My favourite ice-cream flavour is ____________.

I love to eat ____________.

 ISBN 978-81-8477-935-6

Note down some more details about yourself. Ask your parents to help you.

Your birth date: ______________________________

Your height: ______________________________

Your weight: ______________________________

The colour of your eyes: ______________________________

The colour of your hair: ______________________________

The languages you can speak and understand: ______________________________

____

I Care...

When someone says hello or waves to you, it is polite to say hello in return.

Find out a little about the person sitting next to you. Ask him or her the following questions and write down the answers.

Name: ______________________________

Age: ______________________________

Birthday: ______________________________

Telephone number: ______________________________

Favourite thing to eat: ______________________________

Favourite ice-cream flavour: ______________________________

Favourite game to play: ______________________________

 ISBN 978-81-8477-935-6

Do you like drawing, reading, watching television or playing with your friends? Draw a picture or paste a photograph of what you like doing most.

Draw a picture or paste a photograph of your best friend.

 ISBN 978-81-8477-935-6

2
MY FAMILY

 ISBN 978-81-8477-935-6

My mother and father are my **parents.** My brother and sister are also a part of my family. They are called my **siblings**. We live in a house with our family. My parents and siblings form a **small family**.

My grandparents, parents, siblings, aunts and uncles and their children form a **large family**.

Factastic

The children of my uncles and aunts are not my siblings. They are my cousins.

This is a small family.

This is a large family.

Draw or paste a picture of your family.

 ISBN 978-81-8477-935-6

We all have different ways of addressing our family members. In Hindi, you call your father's father *dada* and your father's mother *dadi*. You call your mother's father *nana* and your mother's mother *nani*.

In Malayalam, you call your father's father *achacha* and your father's mother *achama*. You call your mother's father *muttacha* and your mother's mother *ammoma*.

Learn More

What do you call your grandparents?

Your mother's mother: ______________________________

Your father's mother: ______________________________

Your mother's father: ______________________________

Your father's father: ______________________________

Explore

Find out what you call your mother and father in French, German and Spanish. Ask your parents to help you with this task.

Circle Time

Why do you think families are important? What is special about your family?

 ISBN 978-81-8477-935-6

ROLES IN THE FAMILY

All the members of a family play different roles. In some families, both parents go out to work and share the household chores. In other families, the father goes out to work and the mother takes care of the house and the family members.

Each family is different and all the members have different, but important roles to play.

I Care...

Everyone should help out with household tasks. Think about the household tasks you can help with.

 ISBN 978-81-8477-935-6

Children help their parents whenever they ask for it.

Sometimes, people outside the family help us to do certain tasks. Such people include the driver, the gardener, the maid and the guard.

Learn More

What are the different roles that your family members perform?

Father: ______________________________

Mother: ______________________________

What role do you play in your family? How do you help out at home?

I help to ______________________________

Explore

Fill in the names and age of the people in your family.

Name: ______________ Age: ______________

Name: ______________ Age: ______________

Name: ______________ Age: ______________

Name: ______________ Age: ______________

The youngest: ______________ The oldest: ______________

 ISBN 978-81-8477-935-6

FAMILY FUN

Every family has fun together in different ways. Some families like going for picnics, others like to listen to music together. What are the things that your family does together for fun?

Tick (✓) the activities you and your family do together. Circle your favourite activity.

Share a hobby

Celebrate together

Make things

Travel

Play

Go to a carnival

 ISBN 978-81-8477-935-6

Quiz Time

1. **Fill in the blanks to complete the sentences.**

a. My mother's mother is my ______________________.

b. My father's mother is my______________________.

c. My mother's father is my______________________.

d. My brothers and sisters are my__________________.

e. My mother and father are my____________________.

2. **Circle the correct option.**

a. I live with my **friends/family**.

b. My brothers and sisters are my **cousins/siblings**.

c. A **small/large** family has grandparents, parents, siblings, aunts, uncles and their children.

d. All members of a family have **similar/different** roles to play.

3. **Answer the questions.**

a. What is a small family?

b. What is a large family?

c. Do you live in a small family or a large one?

 ISBN 978-81-8477-935-6

3
My Neighbourhood

The area around my house is called my **neighbourhood**. People who live near my house are my **neighbours**. There are places in my neighbourhood that my family and my neighbours find useful.

School

I go to study in a school. Teachers in the school teach me how to read and write. The head of a school is called the **principal**.

I Care...

It is important to keep our neighbourhood clean.

 ISBN 978-81-8477-935-6

In most schools, there are special rooms called classrooms, where teachers teach their students. In many schools, there are playgrounds where children can play sports.

We wear special clothes to school. This is called a **uniform**.

Which of these things can you see in your classroom?

dustbin	☐	clock	☐
blackboard	☐	tree	☐
table	☐	calendar	☐
scissors	☐	pen	☐
pencil	☐	bag	☐
books	☐	scale	☐
watering can	☐	candle	☐
comb	☐	chair	☐

Safety at school. Do you:

	Yes	No
• push friends in the corridors?	☐	☐
• inform the teacher if someone is hurt?	☐	☐
• run on the stairs and in corridors?	☐	☐

 ISBN 978-81-8477-935-6

Explore

Circle the places and things you see on your way to school.

 ISBN 978-81-8477-935-6

MARKET

I go to the market to buy things. A market has many shops. Some shops sell food items such as fruits, vegetables and milk. Other shops sell groceries, clothes or electric items.

Explore

Go shopping with your parents. Observe all the things you see in the market. Write down any three things that your parents bought at the market and their price.

Things we bought	Price

 ISBN 978-81-8477-935-6

PARK

I go to play in the park with my friends. A park usually has swings and slides.

HOSPITAL

A hospital is a place where we go when we are not feeling well or have hurt ourselves. Doctors and nurses in a hospital take care of us, give us medicines and help us get better.

POST OFFICE

I go to the post office to post letters and parcels.

Postal workers, who work in post offices, deliver letters and parcels to people's homes.

POLICE STATION

A police station is where police officers work. They help to make our neighbourhood safe.

 ISBN 978-81-8477-935-6

FIRE STATION

The material required to stop or control a fire is kept in a fire station. Firefighters are trained to control fires. We call a fire station in case a fire breaks out. The moment a fire is reported, firefighters rush off in fire engines to help put out the fire.

Explore

It is always useful to have the contact numbers and addresses of certain places in your neighbourhood handy. Complete the following table. You can ask your parents to help you get this information.

	Name of the person to contact	Phone number	Address
Neighbour			
Neighbour			
Police station			
Hospital			
Bakery			
Grocery store			

 ISBN 978-81-8477-935-6

Circle Time

Share with your friends what you see in your neighbourhood. Which of these do you see?

houses park school post office market hospital

Quiz Time

1. A good neighbourhood has places that help make life easy for us. How well do you know your neighbourhood? Answer the questions by pasting the correct stickers in the boxes. The stickers are provided on the sticker sheet.

a. Where do you go to buy fruits, vegetables, milk, groceries, clothes or electric items?

b. Where do you go to play with friends on swings and slides?

 ISBN 978-81-8477-935-6

c. Where do you find fire-fighting equipment and firefighters?

d. Where do police officers work?

e. Where do you go to post letters and parcels?

f. Where do you go when you are not feeling well or have hurt yourself?

 ISBN 978-81-8477-935-6

2. Find the names of four neighbourhood places hidden in the word grid.

park school hospital post office

d	f	h	j	y	c	s	r	p
s	n	m	l	o	d	f	n	o
c	e	x	a	m	g	t	n	s
h	o	s	p	i	t	a	l	t
o	u	p	a	r	k	j	l	o
o	i	r	d	v	j	k	k	f
l	k	f	x	h	d	h	w	f
t	m	h	s	j	s	s	e	i
f	g	n	c	n	c	j	t	c
x	g	h	v	t	v	k	y	e

 ISBN 978-81-8477-935-6

3. Indicate whether the following statements are true (T) or false (F).

a. Postal workers deliver letters and parcels. ☐

b. A nurse works in a market. ☐

c. We go to the police station when we are not feeling well. ☐

d. Shops sell items such as fruits, vegetables and milk. ☐

e. Firefighters are trained to fight fires. ☐

4. Answer the questions.

a. What is a neighbourhood?

b. Who keeps the neighbourhood safe?

c. Who teaches in a school?

d. Who is the head of a school?

e. What do nurses do?

f. What are the three places every neighbourhood should have?

 ISBN 978-81-8477-935-6

4
COMMUNITY HELPERS

Community helpers are people who help us in our neighbourhood. We depend on them to do the tasks that we are not able to do ourselves.

A **postal worker** delivers letters and parcels to us.

A **watchman** helps guard schools, homes and shops.

Factastic

K. Padmakshi Amma was the first woman postal worker of India. She started working in 1959 at the Trivandrum Postal Division.

 ISBN 978-81-8477-935-6

A **gardener** helps take care of gardens.

A **baker** bakes breads, cakes and cookies.

I Care...

We must always remember to be polite to our community helpers.

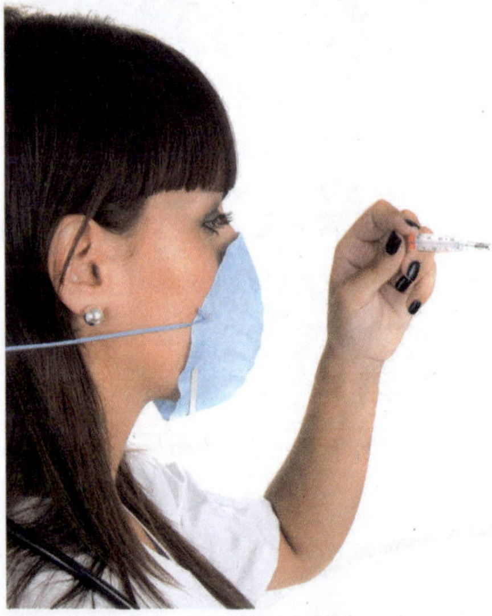

Nurses help doctors to provide medicines and care when we are unwell.

The **garbage collector** collects all the garbage from our homes and makes sure that the streets are clean.

 ISBN 978-81-8477-935-6

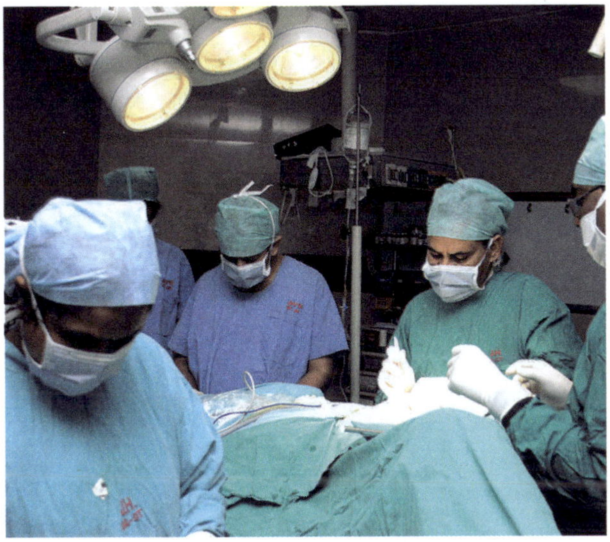

A **doctor** examines us when we are sick. We also go to the doctor for regular check-ups and vaccinations.

A **barber** gives us a haircut when we need one.

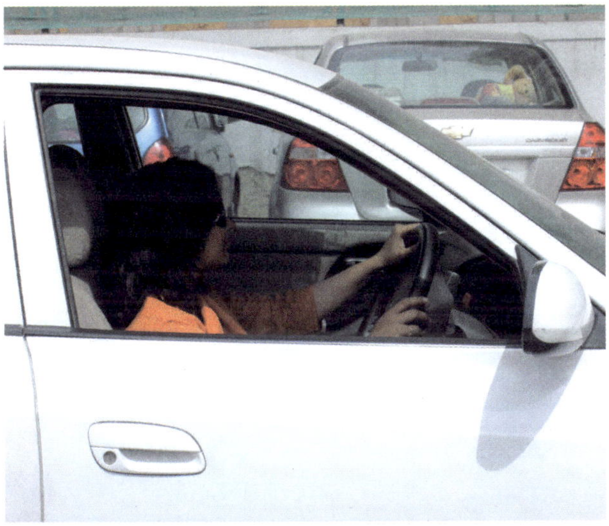

A **driver** drives a bus or car and takes us from one place to another.

The **traffic police** helps manage the traffic on the roads and ensures that nobody breaks traffic rules.

 ISBN 978-81-8477-935-6

Learn More

Draw lines to match the tools to the community helpers who use them.

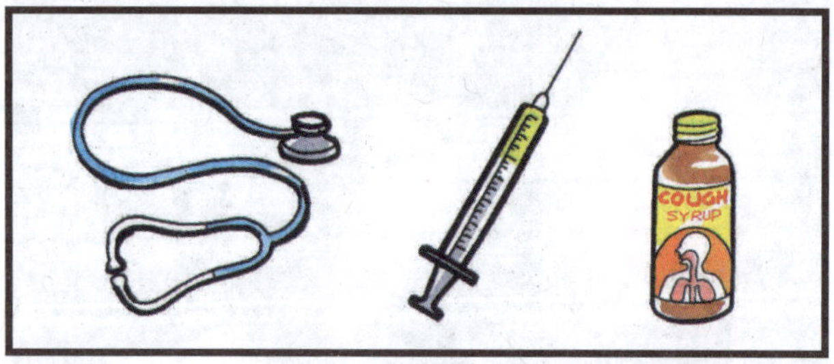

• barber

• doctor

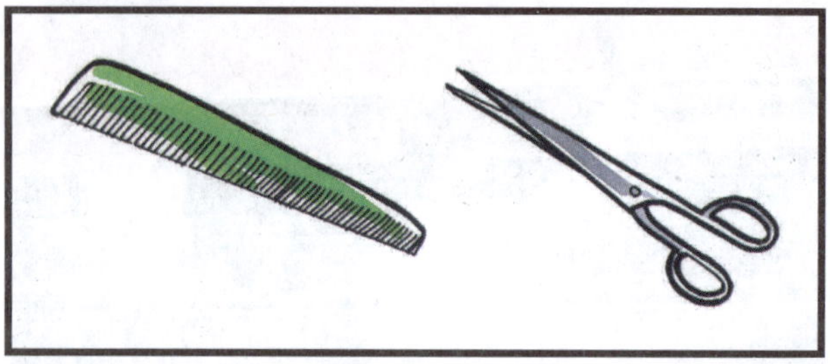

• carpenter

• baker

Explore

Can you think of any other community helpers? List them.

 ISBN 978-81-8477-935-6

Explore

Have a fancy dress party in class. Dress up as your favourite community helper and act out what he or she does.

Quiz Time

1. Circle the correct answer.

a. The **driver/watchman** guards our buildings.

b. The **postman/gardener** takes care of plants.

c. The **doctor/traffic police** manages the traffic on the road.

d. The **gardener/doctor** takes care of us when we are unwell.

2. Who will help us if:

a. there is a fire? ____________________

b. we have fever? ____________________

c. we want to buy cakes and cookies? ____________________

d. we are waiting to receive a letter? ____________________

e. we want to get a haircut? ____________________

3. Answer the questions.

a. Who is a community helper?

b. What does a nurse do?

c. How does the garbage collector help us?

 ISBN 978-81-8477-935-6

5
Religious Festivals

India is known as the land of festivals. A festival is the time for religious or other celebrations. People of different religions celebrate different festivals. Some of the popular celebrations are discussed in this unit.

Dussehra

Dussehra is an important Hindu festival. It marks the victory of Lord Rama over the demon-king, Ravana. Effigies of Ravana, his brother Kumbhakarna and his son Meghanad are burnt as a symbol of victory of good over evil.

Factastic

The Dussehra of Mysore or Mysore Dassara is a ten-day festival, ending with a march of decorated elephants through the city.

 ISBN 978-81-8477-935-6

Durga Puja

Durga Puja is a festival of the Bengalis. It is a ten-day festival. The idol of Goddess Durga is worshipped for nine days and is immersed in the river on the tenth day.

Factastic

Durga Puja is celebrated in Bengal at the same time as Dussehra and Navaratri are celebrated in other parts of India.

Diwali

Diwali is celebrated twenty days after Dussehra.

Diwali is known as the festival of lights. People clean their homes and decorate them with candles and diyas. They distribute sweets and gifts. People light firecrackers. Prayers are offered to Lakshmi, the goddess of wealth.

Factastic

Diwali comes from the word *Deepavali*, which means a row of lights. According to Hindu mythology, this festival is celebrated to mark the return of King Rama to Ayodhya after fourteen years of exile.

 ISBN 978-81-8477-935-6

Circle Time

Have a discussion with your classmates about your favourite festival. Talk about what you like doing on this festival.

Explore

What do you do on Diwali? Tick (✓) the correct box.

	Yes	No
Burst noisy crackers that give out a lot of smoke.	☐	☐
Light sparklers and diyas with an adult.	☐	☐
Wear well-fitted, cotton clothes.	☐	☐
Visit friends and relatives.	☐	☐
Eat lots of sweets.	☐	☐
Decorate your house.	☐	☐

I Care...

While celebrating any festival, we must make sure that we do not disturb others.

Holi

Holi is one of the most popular Hindu festivals. It is the festival of colours. People put coloured powder and water on one another and eat sweets on Holi.

 ISBN 978-81-8477-935-6

Christmas

Christmas is the most important festival for Christians all over the world. It is celebrated on 25 December every year and marks the birth of Jesus Christ. People decorate their homes, sing carols and set up Christmas trees. Children receive presents from family and friends on Christmas.

Eid-ul-Fitr

Eid is the most important festival for Muslims and is celebrated at the end of the holy month of Ramadan. People wear new clothes on this day and visit mosques to offer prayers.

Factastic

Eid-ul-Fitr means time to break the fast. Muslims wish all their near and dear ones 'Eid Mubarak' on Eid-ul-Fitr. Children receive gifts, known as **Eidi**, from their relatives.

 ISBN 978-81-8477-935-6

GURUPURAB

Gurupurab is a festival celebrated by Sikhs. It marks the birthday of Guru Nanak, the founder of the Sikh religion. Prayers are offered at the gurudwara. People decorate their homes with candles and lights.

Gurupurab is also known as Guru Nanak Jayanti.

Factastic

On Gurupurab, the Guru Granth Sahib, the holy book of the Sikhs, is recited continuously in gurudwaras. This is known as the Akhand Path. Processions are taken out, free langars (meals) are arranged and prasad (holy food) is distributed.

Learn More

Look at the calendar and find the dates on which these festivals will be celebrated this year.

Dussehra ______________________

Diwali ______________________

Holi ______________________

Eid-ul-Fitr ______________________

Christmas ______________________

Gurupurab ______________________

 ISBN 978-81-8477-935-6

Explore

Make a card for your favourite festival. Give this card to your teacher or parent.

Quiz Time

1. Fill in the blanks with the correct words from the brackets.

a. We pray to Goddess ______________________ on Diwali (Lakshmi/Saraswati).

b. ______________________ is the most important festival for Muslims (Gurupurab/Eid-ul-Fitr).

c. We celebrate Christmas on ______________________ every year (15 August/25 December).

d. ______________________ is also known as Guru Nanak Jayanti (Gurupurab/Holi).

2. Answer the questions.

a. Which Indian festival is known as the festival of colours?

b. Whose birth is celebrated on Christmas?

c. Where do Sikhs go to offer prayers?

d. Which Indian festival is known as the festival of lights?

 ISBN 978-81-8477-935-6

6

NATIONAL HOLIDAYS

In India, we celebrate a number of events that are of special importance to our nation. The most important of these are Independence Day, Republic Day and Gandhi Jayanti. We have a national holiday on these days. Apart from these, the other events we celebrate in India are Teacher's Day and Children's Day.

Different countries celebrate different national holidays.

INDEPENDENCE DAY

Red Fort, Delhi

On 15 August 1947, India got freedom from British rule. Hence, Indians celebrate Independence Day on 15 August every year. The Prime Minister of India hoists the national flag at the Red Fort in Delhi and makes a speech in which the achievements and plans of the government are discussed.

We all salute the flag and sing the national anthem on this day.

 ISBN 978-81-8477-935-6

Republic Day

Republic Day parade

We celebrate Republic Day on 26 January every year. The Republic Day parade takes place at Rajpath in Delhi. Men and women from the army, navy and air force take part in the parade. The President of India takes the salute at the parade. All the states also participate in the parade.

Factastic

Do you know why the Indian flag is orange, white and green in colour? The colour saffron (orange) stands for patriotism, white stands for simplicity, purity and peace, and green symbolises agriculture and prosperity. The navy blue wheel in the centre is the Ashoka Chakra, the wheel of progress.

Learn More

Draw the flag of India.

I Care...

We must always show respect for our national flag. Never throw the national flag on the ground or fly it upside down.

 ISBN 978-81-8477-935-6

Gandhi Jayanti

Mahatma Gandhi

Mohandas Karamchand Gandhi, also known as Mahatma Gandhi, was born on 2 October 1869 at Porbandar, Gujarat. This day is celebrated as Gandhi Jayanti in his honour. Gandhiji played a very big role in helping India gain independence. We fondly call him *Bapu*.

Children's Day

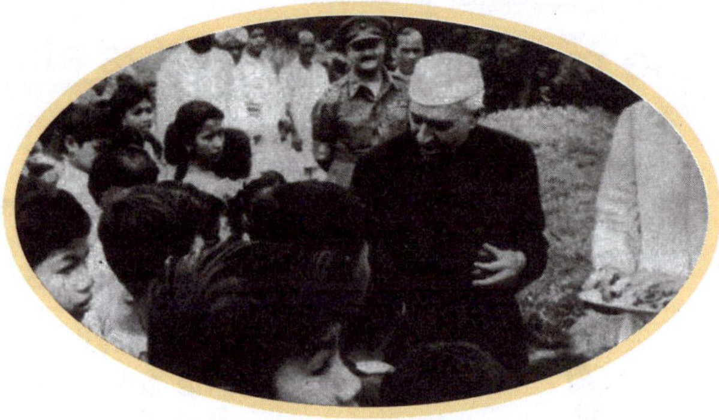

Jawaharlal Nehru

We celebrate Children's Day on 14 November every year. India's first Prime Minister, Jawaharlal Nehru, was born on 14 November 1889. He was very fond of children, hence his birthday is celebrated as Children's Day.

Teacher's Day

Dr S. Radhakrishnan

Dr S. Radhakrishnan was India's former President and a very famous teacher. We celebrate 5 September as Teacher's Day in his honour.

Explore

Find out the names of the current Prime Minister and President of India.

______________________ ______________________

 ISBN 978-81-8477-935-6

Quiz Time

1. Fill in the blanks to complete the sentences.

a. Republic Day is celebrated on ______________________.

b. Independence Day is celebrated on ______________________.

c. ______________________ is celebrated on 2 October.

d. ______________________ is celebrated as Children's Day.

e. 5 September is celebrated as ______________________.

2. Indicate whether the following statements are true (T) or false (F).

a. Children's Day is celebrated on 14 February every year. ☐

b. Mahatma Gandhi was fondly known as Chacha. ☐

c. We celebrate Teacher's Day on 5 September every year. ☐

d. The Prime Minister of India takes the salute at the Republic Day parade. ☐

e. The colour white in the Indian flag stands for purity and peace. ☐

3. Answer the questions.

a. Why do we celebrate Children's Day?

b. What happens in Delhi on Republic Day?

c. What does the colour green stand for in our national flag?

d. Where is the Red Fort?

 ISBN 978-81-8477-935-6

7

Clothes

We need clothes to cover our bodies, protect ourselves from hot or cold weather, from rain and wind. Clothes can be made of different materials such as cotton, wool, silk, nylon and even plastic.

Types of Clothes

We wear different clothes depending on the occasion, the season or the part of the country we live in.

Cotton clothes keep us comfortable in summer. They absorb sweat and keep our body cool.

Pictures of some summer clothes are given below. Tick (✓) the ones you wear.

 ISBN 978-81-8477-935-6

Woollen clothes are made from wool, which is thick, and keep us warm.

Pictures of some winter clothes are given below. Tick (✓) the ones you wear.

I Care...

Donate clothes and shoes that you have outgrown but are still in a good condition.

☐

☐

☐

☐

☐

☐

 ISBN 978-81-8477-935-6

Certain items protect us from weather conditions. These include caps, mufflers, gloves and sunglasses.

In the rainy season, we keep ourselves dry by wearing raincoats, gumboots and by using umbrellas.

People wear different kinds of clothes in different parts of the country. In the hills, people wear warm woollen clothes. In the desert, people wear light-coloured clothes. Near the sea, people wear cotton clothes.

Factastic

Animals and birds do not wear clothes. They have fur, oily skin, fat deposits under the skin or water-proof feathers that protect them from the cold and rain.

 ISBN 978-81-8477-935-6

Circle Time

We wear different clothes for different occasions. Have a discussion with your classmates about different types of clothes. After your discussion, write down what clothes you will wear when you

- go to a beach. ________________ ________________
- go to a party. ________________ ________________
- go to school. ________________ ________________
- go to a place of worship. ________________ ________________
- go to the playground. ________________ ________________

Learn More

These children are dressed according to a particular season. Name the season and list two items of clothing worn in each season.

Season ________________ ________________ ________________

Items of clothing ________________ ________________ ________________

 ISBN 978-81-8477-935-6

Quiz Time

1. Unscramble the letters to complete the sentences.

a. Animals have ______________ (RUF) to keep them warm.

b. We wear ______________ (TOTCON) clothes in summers.

c. Cotton clothes absorb ______________ (ATSEW).

d. A raincoat protects us from ______________ (NIAR).

2. Draw lines and match the following.

a.	Shoes •	• School bag
b.	Shirt •	• Gloves
c.	Sweater •	• Socks
d.	Gumboots •	• Trousers
e.	School uniform •	• Raincoat

3. Answer the questions.

a. What kind of clothes do we wear to keep our body cool?

b. What do we wear to keep our hands warm in winter?

c. What do we wear on our feet in the rainy season?

 ISBN 978-81-8477-935-6

8

Shelter

A house protects us from the hot sun, the cold winter and the rain. It also keeps people and things safe.

Factastic

Animals also have houses to live in.

nest

Birds make nests.

den

Lions live in dens.

hive

Bees make homes known as hives.

Learn More

Find out what materials were used to build your house.

____________________ ____________________

____________________ ____________________

 ISBN 978-81-8477-935-6

Types of Houses

Temporary houses are made of mud, dried grass or straw in villages and plastic, straw or tin in and around cities. These houses are usually weak. They are known as *kuccha* houses.

Permanent houses are made of brick, stone, cement and steel rods. These houses are strong. They are known as *pucca* houses.

Some people live in single-family houses, while others live in apartments. Some housing complexes may have a few apartments while others may have hundreds of apartments.

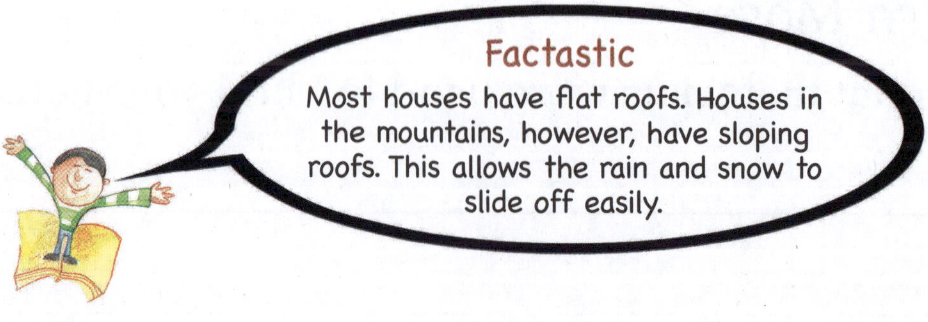

 ISBN 978-81-8477-935-6

Unique Houses

A **houseboat** is a boat with rooms. It is usually made of wood and is able to float on water.

A **tent** is made of sheets of fabric or other material attached to a frame of poles or to a supporting rope.

Some people live in special kinds of houses, such as **trailers** and **caravans**, which are movable.

Factastic

Tree houses are constructed among the branches of trees and are raised above the ground. They can be used for recreation, habitation or as a temporary retreat.

Circle Time

What kind of house would you like to live in if you had a choice between a treehouse, houseboat, caravan or an apartment? Why? Discuss with your class.

 ISBN 978-81-8477-935-6

Parts of a House

The house we live in is called our home. A good home must have windows to let in fresh air and sunlight. Without fresh air, we can fall sick. We need sunlight as it helps kill germs in the air.

Our homes may be big and have several rooms, or small with a few rooms. Each room is used for some activity.

The kitchen is where food is prepared.

The living room is where we sit together or meet guests.

The dining room is where we eat meals.

A bedroom is where we rest and sleep.

I Care...

We should not waste water and electricity. Turn off water taps and electrical switches when not in use.

 ISBN 978-81-8477-935-6

A study is where we read or work.

A bathroom is where we bathe.

Learn More

Is an igloo, tent or skyscraper suitable in different weather conditions?

Tick (✓) where it means suitable for that weather and cross (✗) where it means unsuitable.

	Hot/Sunny	Cold	Windy	Rainy	Snowy

 ISBN 978-81-8477-935-6

Quiz Time

1. In which room will you find these items?

____

____

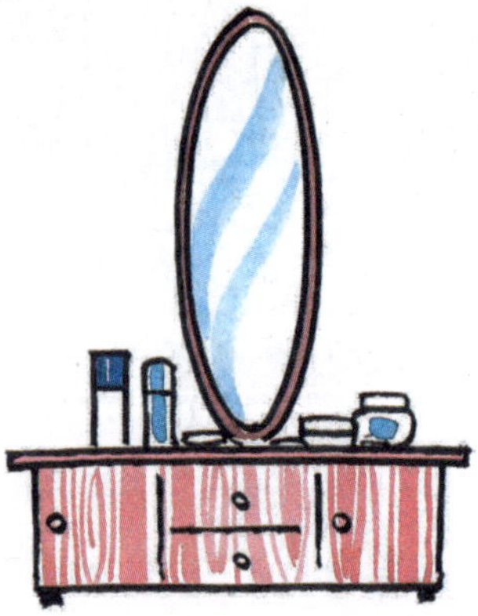

____

____

____

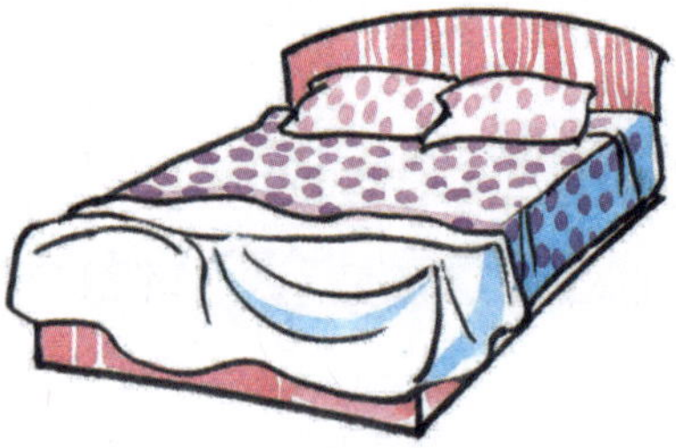

____

2. Fill in the blanks to complete the sentences.

a. We bathe in the ______________.

b. A permanent house is also known as a ______________ house.

c. We cook food in the ______________.

d. Most houses have ______________ roofs.

e. A good home must have windows that let in fresh air and ______________.

 ISBN 978-81-8477-935-6

9
Good Habits and Safety

We must learn to love and respect everyone and everything around us.

We must greet those we meet with a smile.

Bengalis say *Nomoshkar*.

Punjabis say *Sat Sri Akal*.

Tamilians say *Vanakkam*.

How do you greet people? ______________________________

 ISBN 978-81-8477-935-6

Good Habits

We should talk to everyone politely.

We must go to bed on time.

We should be kind to animals.

We must always wash our hands before eating.

We must switch off the lights and fans when we leave a room.

We must eat our meals on time and must not waste food.

We must put away our toys after playing.

We must brush our teeth twice a day.

 ISBN 978-81-8477-935-6

How to Live Safely

Safety means being safe from danger, risk or injury.

There are many things around us that may not be safe and could cause harm. We need to be careful with them. Read the sentences given below carefully. Tick (✓) the correct boxes.

Safety at home	Yes	No
Play with sharp objects	☐	☐
Open the door to strangers	☐	☐
Play near the gas stove or heater	☐	☐
Do not play with electric switches and plugs	☐	☐
Leave toys on the floor after playing	☐	☐

Safety at school	Yes	No
Push friends in the playground	☐	☐
Inform the teacher if someone is hurt	☐	☐
Run on the stairs and in the corridors	☐	☐

Safety on the school bus	Yes	No
Get on and off a moving bus	☐	☐
Wait for turn while getting on and off the bus	☐	☐
Lean out of the windows	☐	☐
Do not stand in a moving bus	☐	☐

 ISBN 978-81-8477-935-6

Safety on the road

Safety on the road	Yes	No
Run and cross the road	☐	☐
Use the footpath while walking on the road	☐	☐
Use the zebra crossing while crossing the road	☐	☐
Cross the road with an adult	☐	☐
Cross the road when traffic has cleared	☐	☐

Learn More

For the next week, see how many times you follow these good habits. Compare your chart with that of your classmates the following week.

	Mon	Tue	Wed	Thur	Fri	Sat	Sun
Brushed your teeth in the morning							
Brushed your teeth at night before going to sleep							
Washed your hands before every meal							
Had all meals on time							

 ISBN 978-81-8477-935-6

	Mon	Tue	Wed	Thur	Fri	Sat	Sun
Went to bed on time							
Made sure to turn off the lights and fans before leaving a room							
Kept your room clean and tidy							

Quiz Time

1. Indicate whether the following statements are true (T) or false (F).

a. We must tease animals. ☐

b. We should not talk to anyone politely. ☐

c. We should sleep late and get up late. ☐

d. We must save electricity and switch off the lights when we leave a room. ☐

e. It is all right to waste some food while eating a meal. ☐

 ISBN 978-81-8477-935-6

2. Colour the correct traffic light for each picture.

'Stop!' says the red light

'Go!' says the green.

'Oh! Be careful and wait!', says the yellow light,

blinking in between.

Colour the RED light if the activity is a dangerous activity that you should not do.

Colour the YELLOW light if you should be careful while doing the activity.

Colour the GREEN light if the activity is a safe one.

 ISBN 978-81-8477-935-6

10 MEANS OF TRANSPORT AND COMMUNICATION

MEANS OF TRANSPORT

We use different means of transport to go from one place to another. We can travel by land, air or water.

On land

On water

By air

I Care...

Walk or use a bicycle rather than drive when the distance is small. This will help save fuel.

 ISBN 978-81-8477-935-6

Factastic

In the past, animals were the most important means of transport. Even today, in small towns and villages, horses, elephants, camels, donkeys, bullocks and ponies carry people as well as goods from one place to another.

On Land

Some vehicles move on land such as cars, buses, trucks, scooters and motorcycles. These run on roads. Trains are also a means of land transport, but they run on rails.

Bus

Car

Motorcycle

Truck

 ISBN 978-81-8477-935-6

On Water

Boats, steamers and ships travel on water. Ships carry passengers and cargo across the oceans and the seas.

Cruise ship

Motor boat

By Air

Air travel is one of the fastest means of transportation. Vehicles which fly include helicopters, rockets and aeroplanes.

Helicopter

Aeroplane

Learn More

Find out the names of the railway station and the airport in your city or nearest to your city.

Airport ______________ Railway station ______________

 ISBN 978-81-8477-935-6

Explore

Ask six of your friends how they travel to school and tick (✓) the appropriate box.

	Name				other
1.					
2.					
3.					
4.					
5.					
6.					

 ISBN 978-81-8477-935-6

Communication

There are many ways to stay in contact with one another. Communication can be one-to-one, as in the case of phone and e-mail, or one-to-many people at the same time, as in the case of TV, radio and newspaper.

The telegraph was the first quick way of relaying messages across long distances. Then, the **telephone** was invented, which became the quickest means of communication. It helps us talk to a person who lives far away. We now have mobile phones that allow us to talk to people and send and receive messages. We can carry a mobile phone wherever we go.

Telephone

Mobile phone

Factastic

In the past, messages were sent by ships, carriages, horses and carrier pigeons. These would take months to reach. Native Americans used smoke signals to send messages.

 ISBN 978-81-8477-935-6

Explore

Make a telephone.

Take two paper cups and make a hole at the bottom of each. Pass a string through the hole in one cup. Tie a knot inside the cup, so that the string cannot come out though the hole. Attach the other end of the same string to the second cup and make another knot.

Bring one of these cups near your mouth, using it like a mouthpiece. Ask your friend to hold the other cup like an earpiece. You can talk while your partner listens to you.

Learn More

Your telephone number is

____________________________.

A computer can also be used for communication. You can send as well as receive information from people located in different parts of the world by e-mail.

People using computers

 ISBN 978-81-8477-935-6

Factastic

E-mail and instant messaging through our computers is the most used method of communication now.

Radio and **television** are the most popular means of communication. They relay programmes based on education, weather, music and entertainment.

Television

Learn More

Your favourite TV channel is ______________.

A person reading a newspaper

Newspapers are the cheapest means of communication. They provide news to a large number of people every morning.

Write the names of the newspaper

that your family reads. ______________

that your neighbours read. ______________

 ISBN 978-81-8477-935-6

Learn More

How would you communicate with the following?

		phone	e-mail	letter
a.	A friend who lives in the same city.	☐	☐	☐
b.	An uncle who lives in another country.	☐	☐	☐
c.	Your grandfather who lives in another city.	☐	☐	☐

Quiz Time

1. Use the words in the box below to fill in the blanks.

trains	cargo	fastest	animals

a. People in villages use ______________________ as a means of transport.

b. Ships carry ______________________ across the oceans and seas.

c. ______________________ run on rails.

d. Air travel is the ______________________ means of transportation.

 ISBN 978-81-8477-935-6

2. Tick (✓) the means of transport you have used.

bus	☐	auto-rickshaw	☐
bicycle	☐	tram	☐
tractor	☐	scooter	☐
train	☐	aeroplane	☐
helicopter	☐	truck	☐

3. Answer in one word.

a. The quickest means of transport.

b. The most popular means of communication.

c. The cheapest means of communication.

d. The quickest means of communication.

e. The earliest means of communication used for relaying messages over long distances.

4. Answer the questions.

a. Why do we need transport?

b. Name three means of land transport.

c. Name three means of water transport.

d. Name three means of air transport.

e. How were messages sent in the past?

 ISBN 978-81-8477-935-6

5. Where do these vehicles travel? Paste **L** for land, **W** for water and **A** for air. The stickers are provided on the sticker sheet.

 ISBN 978-81-8477-935-6

 ISBN 978-81-8477-935-6

11 DIRECTIONS

If you stand straight, you will find that you can move your arm on four sides: front, back, up and down.

The four main directions are **north**, **south**, **east** and **west**. The Sun rises in the east and sets in the west.

A compass helps us to identify directions. The needle of a compass always points north.

DIRECTIONS

There are different ways to get to one place. To go somewhere, we need to know the directions.

When we say that a place is to the left or to the right or it is up the street or down the street, we are giving directions. Without them, we can get lost.

 ISBN 978-81-8477-935-6

A map is a drawing that shows us a place, a neighbourhood or a city. We use it to find our way.

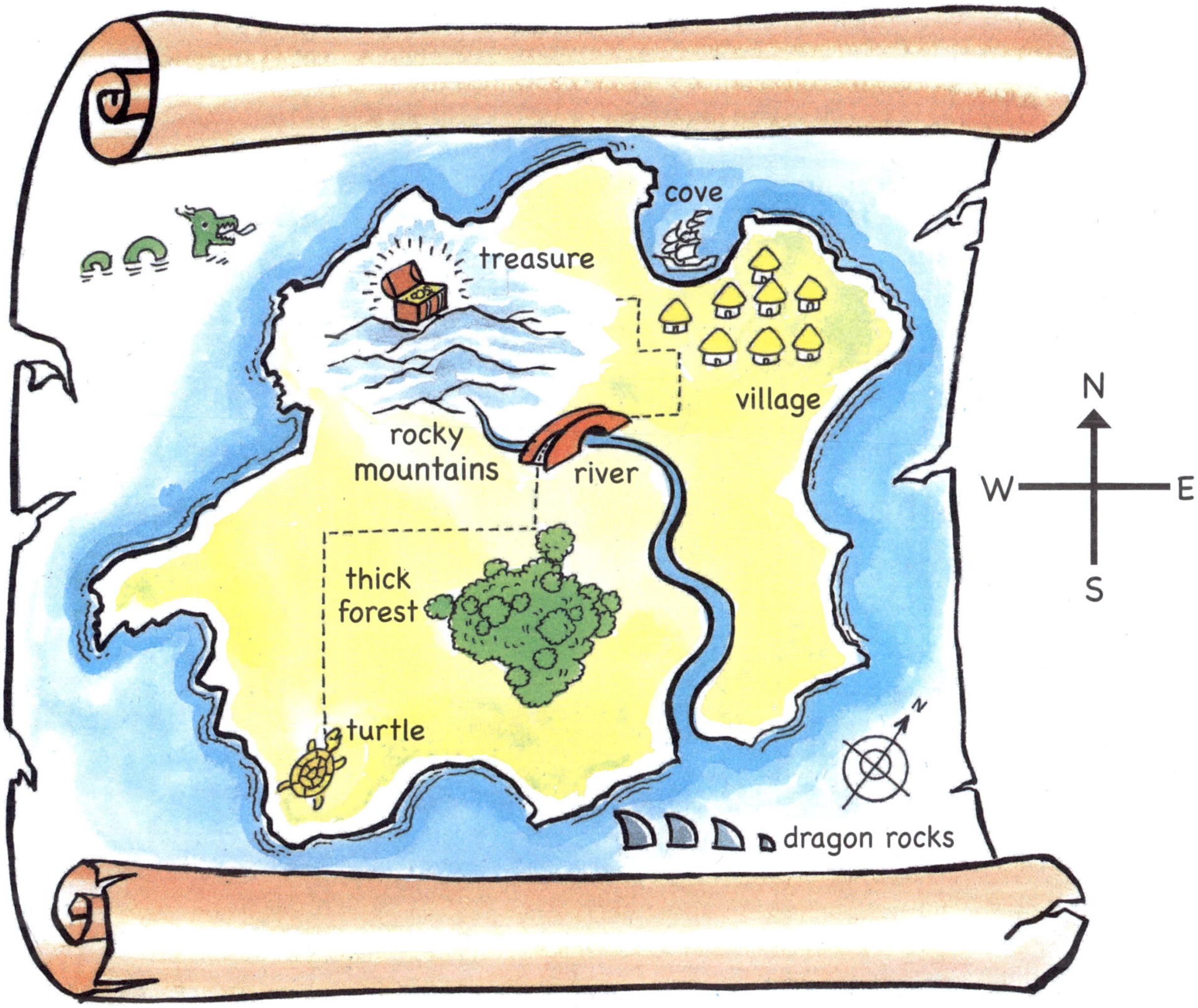

Study the map carefully and give the turtle directions to reach the treasure. You can use the short forms given below.

I Care...

When giving someone directions, be sure to mention important landmarks. This will help them locate places quickly.

U = up ↑ ____________________

L = left ← ____________________

R = right → ____________________

D = down ↓ ____________________

 ISBN 978-81-8477-935-6

Learn More

Draw a map of the route you take from your house to school. Mark all the important landmarks that you see on your way.

Quiz Time

1. Rani lives in Fun City. Her house is on Green Avenue. Find her house. Fill in the blanks with the correct words from the brackets.

a. To get to the park, Rani goes ________ (west/east/south).

b. The mall is to the ________ of Rani's house (north/south/west).

c. The post office is to the ________ of the mall (south/east/west).

d. To go to school, Rani goes ________ (south/north/east).

 ISBN 978-81-8477-935-6